Battle In The Sea: How To Tackle Spiritual Warfare And Win The Battle

Johannes Tefo

Published by Johannes Tefo, 2024.

Also by Johannes Tefo

Family spiritual Warfare Books
Youth's Guide To Spiritual Warfare
A Women's Guide To Spiritual Warfare

Standalone
Deliver Your Soul From Evil
Overcoming Spirit Of Stagnation
The 24: Prophetic Word For This Season 2024 And Beyond
Michael For Warfare
Territorial Spirits: Overcome Evil Strongholds in Your Life And
Take Over Your Community With Strategic Warfare And
Winning Prayers
Prayers Against Suicide Spirit
Spiritual Warfare When Enough is Enough
Identity In Christ
Prayers Against Satanic Networks
The Workplace You Need: Spiritual Warfare Prayers That
Silence Evil Powers At Your Workplace.

Deliverance From Mind Control: Be Free And Delivered From
Every Marine Demons Of Mind Control
Times Getting Hard: Scriptures Of Comfort For Hard Days
Battle In The Sea: How To Tackle Spiritual Warfare And Win
The Battle

Table of Contents

I dedicate this book to those who are battling with marine powers.

I pray that the grace of GOD abounds in your life!

Introduction.

It's funny I only learned about the marine kingdom in the Pentecostal churches. All along, I had no idea what it was. However, the church I was attending, unknowingly used to partake in the things of the marine world. For instance, like going to the rivers and mountains to fetch water for pastors to bless or anoint them. Without a doubt, 70 percent of church rituals include water. Bear in mind, that there is nothing wrong with water. Water is life.

My argument is that we have ritualized water and oil within churches to the point that it is now seen as a church culture. I know that faith healing is moved by faith and revelation. Jesus Christ, the perfector of souls, used soil or mud for healing the blind man. Peter's shadow used to heal people when passing by. Apostle Paul had also a strange way of healing people. He was highly anointed by the Most High that his handkerchief was anointed to heal.

I believe these brothers adhered to the call of the Holy Spirit. They were sensitive to be able to discern when the Holy Spirit was speaking. Healing is an act of faith, and with prophetic ears, one can do valiant things in the kingdom business by moving when God is moving.

John 14:12 Verily, verily, I say unto you, He that believeth on me, the works that I
do shall he do also; and greater works than these shall he do; because I go unto
my Father.

2

This verse implies that all believers in Christ have the authority and power to do greater works than Christ. I believe in miracle healing, and I believe in the great exploitation of deliverances and breakthroughs. I also believe in the great anointing that has been transferred to the church. since it is the last days, God always raises the standard when Satan lifts up.

However, the enemy, Satan, has infiltrated our space, walking around like a roaring lion to devour souls. There is a kingdom under the sea that many think it's just a fiction or a myth. This kingdom is called the marine kingdom. The supplier of power, fame, and money to so many priests, prophets, and pastors that we have today.

We have seen, that some of the anointing water and oil essentials, come from the marine kingdom. There is an anointing from God, and there is also the perverted anointing from the kingdom of darkness.

King Soul is an example to show us that when the Holy Spirit lifts up from you, other spirits come in. A man's body cannot be left uninhabited, if it is not the Holy Spirit, it is the demons that blind us from seeing the light of the truth of God. Some of the traditions that we are used to in the church are just traditions, and they have nothing to do with God. We ought to move from church culture to church faith. Faith in God births dreams into reality.

The promises of God are handpicked through unshakable faith in Christ. This kingdom, Marine, is a manipulative and deadly government ruled by the Devil himself. He is the god of this world, and he sits at the high places of this world, he has also strategized a water kingdom that rules every territory of this world. He only thrives because his works are in the darkness. He thrives because many believers and people general all over the world, do not believe he exists.

In light of the scriptures, and from personal experience, Satan exists, and many high-profile people we honor have made a pact with him. Presidents have sold their nations for money, power, and fame. Celebrities have sold their morality for fame. Some religious leaders have also donated souls to this kingdom in exchange for money, power, and fame.

We have three domains of Satan: The Marine kingdom under the sea, high places (spiritual wickedness in the heavenly) this is the space above the clouds, and the underworld. Many are familiar with Satan ruling the underworld. To this day, some also believe that he lives in hell. His time has not come yet, he travels around the world, kingdoms, and dimensions. He is the devouring lion, however, this is the nature that he does not reveal when he manifests himself to people. He comes as the angel of light, that, if you don't have the gifts to discern spirits, you will be lured into his gimmicks and tricks.

God is all-powerful and has a diverse of healing anointing and powers to the church. Bear in mind, I have nothing against water healing, as a way of faith healing. However, through personal experience, thorough study of the Word, and in-depth research about this kingdom, I have observed that water is its trademark. Water is life. Water sustains the earth. Water is the foundation of the earth. Therefore, the devil decided to have his throne in the sea to rule and destroy humanity.

I am talking about the Devil because he is the main guy who strategically brought order in his kingdom, placing principalities, powers, rulers, and dominion high-ranking demons in every sector of this world, from every little village to the great cities. It

4

sounds as if I'm giving him credit but I am not. It is just for your awareness. You have to study the enemy you are contending with for a sure victory. And you also have to know who you are, and where you stand.

We stand behind the rock. The rock is CHRIST. Just as Moses had to stand on the cliff of the rock to see the back of the glory of God, we are to be under the authority of JESUS CHRIST for our protection.

We will get deeper into this kingdom of darkness. Warriors of CHRIST always get a glimpse of the kingdom of Satan to be able to wage strategic spiritual warfare for the church. Joshua before conquering Jericho, had to send spies to study the land and the pattern of the land. This is what I believe every warrior will do. You cannot fight what you do not know and expect to be triumphant. Especially when you are dealing with highest highest-ranking principalities. Or even the highest level of occult.

Early in the beginning of the book of Genesis, we are introduced to the deceiver, Satan. Before any man can rise, he has to defeat his foes. JESUS had to defeat the Devil before his ministry could take off. Even as a God-man, he had to endure what his brothers and sisters were going through in their faith life daily. He is our perfect example in all things.

I am writing this book from personal experience and personal study of the Word of God. For more than 10 years, I used to be a member of a certain church in South Africa that was using water rituals as a form of faith healing. And of course, other essentials such as oil, branded teas, and anointed cosmetics for administering healing and deliverance.

Almost, 70 percent of the Pentecostal charismatic movement rests on these products for healing. It is more like a shifted faith from the source to an object as a form of healing and deliverance. Many trust these things more than prayer.

And I have found out that, many of the new healing products come from the marine world.

James 5:14 Is any sick among you? let him call for the elders of the church; and let

them pray over him, anointing him with oil in the name of the Lord:

15 And the prayer of faith shall save the sick, and the Lord shall raise him

up; and if he have committed sins, they shall be forgiven him.

But someone with argue that oil is there in the bible for ministering healing right? Yeah, but you cannot make a whole new doctrine of it. Apostle Paul could not whenever someone needs healing, pull out his handkerchief. This would leave the impression that nothing can heal except handkerchiefs. Boxing the power of the Holy Spirit in a container. JESUS could heal blindness with mud because He was sensitive to the Holy Spirit. He moved when the Holy Spirit moved. That is why the body of CHRIST has to highly uphold the gift of the discerning spirit.

This is the prophetic gift that allows you to discern between the move of God and the move of the enemy. It all comes down to faith and being sensible to the voice of the Holy Spirit of God. The lack of patience led many prophets and pastors to seek power from the marine world. This is big on African soil. Many double up with power from the water—invoking the spirits of mermaids, mythical creatures, and all types of snake creatures for wealth, healing, divination, and power.

Started on the right foot, and ended up on the wrong side of the route.

> Nahum 3:1-3: *"Woe to the bloody city! it is all full of lies and robbery; the prey departeth not; The noise of a whip, and the noise of the raffling of the wheels, and of the pransing horses, and of the jumping chariots. The horseman lifteth up both the bright sword and the glittering spear: and there is a multitude of slain, and a great number of carcases; and there is none end of their corpses; they stumble upon their corpses:"*

Many nations and many lives will not advance unless this is dealt with. It is to be noted that practically in all nations there are people who worshiped bodies of water. These spirits are proud, mean, wicked, heartless, and stubborn. They try to control trade and commerce.

70% of the world is covered with water; the atmosphere has a greater percentage of water and the land is dependent on water to survive. Above all, MAN, the apex of God's creation contains 70% water. This gives them influence over mankind. Moreover, the human race cannot do without water (water use-ages). This might sound strange but the truth is - every country, state, city, town or village has a territorial presence that defines the course of events within the territory.

The land, air, and sea are the three demonic bases through which Satan advances his agenda on the earth (Genesis 1:28; Revelation 10:1-10).

Marine spirits are the princes and princesses of the sea (Ezekiel 26:16). These class of demons are responsible for all the whoredomness in our world, they perpetuate the highest level of wickedness against mankind in the form of filthiness, defilements, sexual bondages, depravity, marital breakups and disillusionments.

Apart from the very visible penetration of Marine spirits in our society today in influencing the music, fashion, and film industries, these spirits also oppress people by coming to have sex with them in their dreams or even claiming to be married to them, resulting in what is called spiritual husband or spiritual wife. This spiritual union eventually becomes a ground for the devil to cut the victims out of their blessings in Christ and keep them in pain and suffering as explained.

BEFORE TIME.

It is with my strong belief that Satan's fall was before time. It was in an eternal realm, where time and space do not matter. In a realm where thoughts speak louder than words. Where the level of your greatness is determined by your light of glory. And it is all due to the grace and mercy of GOD.

Genesis 1:1 In the beginning God created the heaven and the earth.

GOD created the earth to be inhabited by man. GOD did not create a faulty earth, as it is written that the earth was without form. GOD is the GOD of perfection. In the beginning, GOD created the heaven and the earth. In Genesis 1:2, there was destruction on earth. I strongly believe there was a gap between Genesis 1:1 and Genesis 1:2.

Genesis 1:2 And the earth was without form, and void; and darkness was upon the face
of the deep. And the Spirit of God moved upon the face of the waters.

The eye-catching words from this scripture are "Without form" and "Void". Without form and void are synonymous with words like "Annulled" "Cancelled" "Invalid" and "Emptiness". We understand that this was before the human race. But food for thought, can GOD create an invalid earth? Void earth? There must have happened something to disrupt the earth between Genesis 1:1 and Genesis 1:2. The CREATOR called the earth into being from nothing. Everything that we see comes from nothing but from the Mighty Word of GOD.

We see the relationship between the CREATOR and CHRIST as the WORD is CHRIST Himself.

John 1:1 In the beginning was the Word, and the Word was with God, and the
Word was God.
2 The same was in the beginning with God.
3 All things were made by him; and without him was not any thing made
that was made.

GOD spoke CHRIST (THE WORD) and The HOLY SPIRIT that was hovering upon the face of the earth empowered the WORD and the WORD manifest—produced fruitful results.

And the Spirit of God moved upon the face of the waters

The FATHER, SON, and HOLY SPIRIT manifested in the beginning.

Psalm 33:9 For he spake, and it was done; he commanded, and it stood fast.

The then world was spoken and commanded out of nothing. Then, there was the fall of Lucifer that brought disruption of the Cosmos and earth. The kingdoms and cities were destroyed. The then civilization experienced the fall of the star from the third heaven.

Ezekiel 28:14 Thou art the anointed cherub that covereth; and I have set thee so: thou
wast upon the holy mountain of God; thou hast walked up and down in the midst
of the stones of fire.

Lucifer had a great honor and authority in the court of discussion in the heavenly realm. He is called the anointed cherub that covereth. He covered the glory of GOD AND WAS Illuminated by the glory. The degree of the light of GOD upon his apparel was great.

thou hast walked up and down in the midst
of the stones of fire.

Not all Angels are in the presence of GOD. Lucifer was meeting with GOD. He knows GOD! Wisdom, knowledge, and understanding were in Him. Apart from him being a worshipper, he had authority over the kingdoms. He also wore various stones like a high priest.

Ezekiel 28:13 Thou hast been in Eden the garden of God; every precious stone was thy
covering, the sardius, topaz, and the diamond, the beryl, the onyx, and the jasper,
the sapphire, the emerald, and the carbuncle, and gold: the workmanship of thy
tabrets and of thy pipes was prepared in thee in the day that thou wast created.

I am writing all of this for you to know who you are dealing with. Many do not know the enemy we are fighting—Satan. In billions of times, he would never love you but use you to perpetrate destruction on earth. The wisdom he corrupted, he is still using today to turn this world into chaos, politically, economically, and socially. Every sector feels the impact of this spirit being.

He still uses music and entertainment to weaken the souls of men. Music is power. Music is spiritual. Behind every song, there is mood, feeling, and spirit. The most important part of yourself is your brain and your subconscious mind. As he is after the minds of men and women, he will use whatever means to get you. Without GOD, we are no match for these beings.

It has to be with honor to exalt the name of the LORD that has delivered many from the spiritual bondage of the Evil One. On your own, you cannot take off the evil blinders, the name of CHRIST will.

The Angels that fell with Lucifer were many, if not millions.

Revelations 12:12 Therefore rejoice, ye heavens, and ye that dwell in them. Woe to the
inhabiters of the earth and of the sea! for the devil is come down unto you,
having great wrath, because he knoweth that he hath but a short time.

The earth and the sea will not have peace for he has descended upon. To persecute the believers in CHRIST. Many of these fallen ones inhabit the sea. The underwater world is another vast kingdom that is against the men and women of the land. Men made a pact with these beings, that they have the right to walk among us.

Recently happened a mysterious thing in our province, near my village, a man appeared in a chief's house complaining about how the people of the village make a lot of noise near the mountain where he lives and that his children are unable to cope with the noise. The mountain is near the road. He threatened the village with the stormy disaster that would destroy the village.

This man was a merman. Half-men, half-fish. However, he disguised himself as a man. This is the undersea man living in the mountains. Mind you, it did happen, there was a serious storm within that week after he left—houses were destroyed, and some people lost their lives. It is still a mystery.

In the last days, we shall see mysterious things and spirit beings shall manifest around the globe. Especially spirit beings like mermaids, mermen, aliens, giants of old, and ancient gods and goddesses shall make a comeback indeed. As It was in the day of Noah, so shall it be with this generation!

The mysteries of this world you can find them in the mountains, oceans, seas, lakes, and rivers. The gods and goddesses have made it their habitation. Ours is in the heaven of heaven on the side of the north. He is the great One!

Stay awake. For we are already in the end times. Be conscious of places like Mountains and oceans. We are not alone. Like in the days of Noah, there were mysterious beings. Trust in the LORD GOD MOST HIGH!

My spiritual experience.

I met the LORD JESUS CHRIST as a young man. I always had dreams, visions, and a deep revelation about CHRIST. By the way, do not let the capital letters of the name of CHRIST take you off. As someone who is a scribe for the LORD, it was revealed to me in a vision to always use capital letters on any divine names of CHRIST. CHRIST is the KING OF KINGS.

As I was saying, way before I even set foot in a church, I had previously revelation of CHRIST. I believe earlier on; it was a testament that I was going to serve the kingdom of God while on this earth. And to tell you the truth, serving the LORD JESUS CHRIST, is getting harder and harder as we go on this journey. I have learned that it is a journey of faith. The journey of the example of Abraham's faith.

There are many times you would have just given up, but, faith kept you on your toes. This was me. As my family was a member of a certain African Initiated Church, a type of messianic church, at the right time I also went there. That is where I learned about marine spirits—and the whole kingdom. The church revolves around water. There is still that Old Testament emblem of water purification, water sprinkling, and holy water drinking especially when you are suffering from misfortunes, illness, and sickness.

During my stay at that church, I was reading the bible but not into it that much. Because I was fascinated by its prophetic ability. You know when you are in the Pentecostal charismatic churches, you are drawn and taken by its energy, especially through praise and worship. Pentecostal brothers are more yielded to spirit life. However, I have witnessed the lack of sound doctrine.

To cut a long story short, I decided to leave the church I am talking about, which I will not mention. But it is one of the biggest churches in South Africa. I have seen behind closed doors, behind the curtains, what these priests, bishops, prophets, and pastors do when no one is looking. Many of them start on the right track but end up straying away because of hunger for power mixed with greed for honor, fame, and money. You can be successful even in the house of God without mixing with strange gods.

When you study the history of ancient Israel from Egypt to this day, they have always mixed with other strange gods and goddesses. And the hand of the ALMIGHTY GOD was so strong over them. Idol worship is an abomination to GOD. We serve a jealous GOD who wouldn't allow other strange gods to take the glory.

I have received a quite number of visions, night visions, dreams, and revelations about the bishop of this church since he has the biggest following. I learned that many like his church, draw powers from the marine world. He mingles with mystical creatures for miracles, healing, and deliverance. Not all spirits come from the LORD. The LORD is that spirit of liberty—the spirit of peace.

Other spirits make noise—there is confusion and fear when you are dealing with them. One of the greatest principality of South African churches is the leviathan. This is one of the deadliest marine dragons under the seas that is brewing the nation with pride, violence, and immoral living.

Leviathan is a counterfeit of the Holy Spirit. An imitation of the work of the Holy Spirit. The priest of this kind uses divination and soothsaying claiming to be prophetic within the church. under this beast, there are other snake spirits such as python—and all serpentine snakes such as Kundalini, masking themselves as the Holy Spirit. This spirit is the king of the sea.

I gave my testimony on one of the books I ever wrote, *Occulthood in Church: First Hand Testimony,* about my journey of how I was unknowingly initiated into the occult within a church. when I am writing this piece, I am writing from personal experience. I also do diligent research, be it scriptures *and* sources from the library.

We are spiritual people living in a world that was founded on spiritual principles. As a spiritual person, you have to know that things don't just happen. It is all about the energy source behind things. Be it angelic or demonic. It is either JESUS or the Devil. It cannot be both—meaning you cannot serve them both.

JESUS is the way, the truth, and life—serve Him only. He is the only way to the heart of GOD. He is your gift to the eternal life, and my gift ticket to the eternal life. There is life beyond what eyes and mind can comprehend.

Fear of the LORD is the beginning of wisdom. At the end of the day, in the name of the LORD, we shall conquer. I am glad you are reading this book as it is an eye-opener and a total deliverance manual to freedom in the LORD.

Battle in the sea.

I titled this book Battle in the Sea because that is where the intense battle is at. The sea is a hot spot for battle—especially spiritual battles. There is a whole different world under the sea that is where the great seat of the Devil is at.

The foundation of the earth is in the sea. Therefore, I believe, the Devil wants to be the foundation of all kinds of evil that is happening around the world. Plus, he is a copycat, in Psalms 24 and 29, it is written that the LORD is upon the floods. This talks about the great authority that the LORD has over all people.

Ezekiel 28:1-3Son of man, say unto the prince of Tyrus, Thus saith the Lord GOD;

Because thine heart is lifted up, and thou hast said, I am a God, I sit in the seat of

God, in the midst of the seas; yet thou art a man, and not God, though thou set

thine heart as the heart of God: 3 Behold, thou art wiser than Daniel; there is no

secret that they can hide from thee:

In the realm of spirit, the sea symbolizes all people of all nation and their languages. We get this idea from the Book of Revelation. As we all know, the Book of Revelation explains itself. Therefore, the LORD is upon the flood, the Psalmist says " *For thou, LORD, art high above all the earth: thou art exalted far above all gods (Psalm 97:9).*

Let the sea roar, and the fulness thereof; the world, and they that dwell therein. 8 Let the floods clap their hands: let the hills be joyful together 9 Before the LORD; for he cometh to judge the earth: with righteousness shall he judge the world, and the people with equity (Psalm 98: 7-8).

The sea must praise the LORD who made it. They that dwell therein must glorify its maker, THE LORD OF HOST!

The beings in the seas are to offer the great LORD praises and honor. But the enemy, Satan, has turned both beast and men away from GOD. The destruction of the fall of Lucifer turned the world into chaos and emptiness. From then on, the serpentine spirit has been after men and women—to turn them away from the will of GOD.

Job 1:6-7 Now there was a day when the sons of God came to present themselves
before the LORD, and Satan came also among them.
7 And the LORD said unto Satan, Whence comest thou? Then Satan
answered the LORD, and said, From going to and fro in the earth, and from
walking up and down in it.

In this passage above, we can see that the Devil had access to the throne of GOD. Since he is the accuser of the brethren, he has to be in the courtroom of GOD to condemn believers before GOD. Thank GOD for his abounding grace and mercy through the blood of CHRIST. We are already on the battlefield contending with the powers of darkness and it is through the grace and the anointing of GOD that breaks every yoke that we shall conquer.

Spirits never get tired. Witches and wizards camp every, they don't miss it. That's why we as believers have to be persistent and walk in endurance faith. We overcome in the name of JESUS CHRIST. We are overcome by the blood of the LAMB. We are overcome by faith. Faith is the most important of all, it opens the ancient journey of righteousness and holiness.

We have three domains; the air, the land, and the sea. Don't get me wrong, evil powers are in the air, land, and sea. I decided to focus on the sea because the sea was before everything. God found the earth upon the sea and the floods.

Psalm 24:1-2 The earth is the LORD's, and the fulness thereof; the world, and they that
dwell therein.
2 For he hath founded it upon the seas, and established it upon the floods.

Psalm 29:10 The LORD sitteth upon the flood; yea, the LORD sitteth King for ever.

The land, air, and sea are the three demonic bases through which Satan advances his agenda on the earth (Genesis 1:28; Revelation 10:1-10). This revelation is a MUST for all watchmen and prayer band leaders. One way to protect the integrity of your city, church, family, and businesses, is to put these demonic bases under check and forbade any advances from them through regular atmospheres of prayers.

Water is spiritual. The spirit of the LORD was hovering upon it. Water is also one of the most important elements. Magicians, Sangomas, witches, and wizards know the power of water. Almost all their rituals are done near the river or lakes. It is only water that can quench the fire. The first judgment was flooded in the days of Noah.

First and foremost, water is important to God, to us, even in the kingdom of the Devil. Thus, the marine kingdom is built in the sea. There are cities in the sea, mansions, and advanced technology the whole kingdom is a replica of this world but in an advanced manner. I also believe that the Devil also tried to replicate what was in heaven in the sea as he was the resident of the heavenlies.

Only in the whole bible, Lucifer is called the anointed Cherubim. He had the honor, authority, power, and fame more than other angels. Cherubim's are the ones close to the throne of God. In heaven, the closer you are to GOD, the greater His countenance upon you. His wisdom, knowledge, and understanding are lightening up upon you. However, he corrupted his wisdom through pride which led to rebellion.

Isaiah 14:12 How art thou fallen from heaven, O Lucifer, son of the morning! how art
thou cut down to the ground, which didst weaken the nations!
13 For thou hast said in thine heart, I will ascend into heaven, I will exalt
my throne above the stars of God: I will sit also upon the mount of the
congregation, in the sides of the north: 14 I will ascend above the heights of the
clouds; I will be like the most High.

Note that Lucifer did not move his mouth or speak, it was his thoughts *"For thou hast said in thine heart".* It is only GOD who knows the heart of men. Through experience and personal encounters with the LORD, I have discovered that in the spirit realm, you don't have to speak with your mouth to say something but your thoughts speak louder than your mouth. The LORD JESUS can speak to your mind to mind without moving His lips. Some people call this telepathy.

As the children of the MOST HIGH, we must renew our minds daily through the power of the Word. I have also found out that you can renew your mind through meditation. Note, godly meditation whereby you let the Word of GOD be your reflection through decrees, proclamation, praise, memorization, etc. nothing as powerful as the mighty Word of God.

As we still dealing with the issue of the fall of the enemy, his heart deceived him. And here we are, having to deal with evil thoughts that he plants in the hearts of men. The same principles of heaven, Satan still uses. However, he uses his wisdom for evil works.

We are blessed with all spiritual blessings in the heavenly places, and one of the greatest gifts, has to be the discerning of spirits, some call it the spirit of discernment. Especially when you are dealing with spiritual powers. Deception is the weapon of the last day against believers, even against the very elect. So, this gift will help with the ability to discern between spirits as we are not supposed to neglect prophecies but scale them. Not all spirits come from the Lord. And marine spirits always camouflage as the angels of light.

The Devil will not come as a horn man with a red suit to deceive but as the angel of light. Most do not know that he is the most beautiful man you will ever see in life. Even after the fall, he can still transform himself into the state of an angel. In times of Job, he even has access to the third heaven, where the throne of GOD is.

Job 1:6-7 Now there was a day when the sons of God came to present themselves
before the LORD, and Satan came also among them.

7 And the LORD said unto Satan, Whence comest thou? Then Satan
answered the LORD, and said, From going to and fro in the earth, and from
walking up and down in it.

Only God was able to perceive him. Though he lost his glory but still has power and the anointing. He was the anointed cherubim in the presence of the Most High to minister through worship and praise. His assignment was in worship. In fact, he led worship in heaven. This happens before time, in the eternal realm. Spirit beings are not confined to the limitation of time.

I saw a night vision, and in that vision, I saw Satan, I just knew in my heart that he was, but he was not a horned vicious man wearing a black gown, no. He was beautiful looking, in his mid-30s, with pipes in his body. The pipes are the instruments that are in him to worship the MOST HIGH GOD. The Psalmist says "Praises comes comely to the upright in the LORD".

Lucifer was music himself. He was not playing for the LORD but instruments in him played for the LORD. That is how powerful GOD is. That is why he is called the anointed Cherubim *"the workmanship of thy tabrets and of thy pipes was prepared in thee in the day that thou wast created".*

The musical instruments were made the day he was created by the MOST HIGH. If you ever feel overwhelmed by the enemy sometimes, just know that he was created. And that you have the CREATOR of all things, who is above all things, and you live forever. We also have the great prince, Angel Michael, who is fighting spiritual rivalries in spirit for you to conquer in all things.

Angel Michael is the helper of humankind during difficult times. As we are approaching the end, Michal shall rise up and manifest himself in special ways to the church. He also has his mighty army of the warriors of the LORD. I wrote the whole book dedicated to Michael for the things I have seen him doing in my life through the grace of GOD. Psalm 91 is our covering as the body of CHRIST, in CHRIST all things work together for good.

Ezekiel 28:13 Thou hast been in Eden the garden of God; every precious stone was thy
covering, the sardius, topaz, and the diamond, the beryl, the onyx, and the jasper,
the sapphire, the emerald, and the carbuncle, and gold: the workmanship of thy
tabrets and of thy pipes was prepared in thee in the day that thou wast created.

We have to talk about the Devil as he is the leader of all fallen angels bringing destruction upon this planet. Diseases, disasters, death, poverty, and other social ills are the result of the evil one. The marine kingdom's mission is destruction and catastrophe for every human being on this planet.

Whether you are good or not, believer or not, spiritual or not, the Devil is your number one biggest enemy. Rage and wrath are his nature. He unleashes his timeless powers—throwing demonic evil arrows at us to weaken our faith in GOD. Your faith is precious to GOD. Whether your faith is strong, weak, or lukewarm, never give up. GOD rewards those who shall endure till the end of time. I pray that the spirit of endurance be upon your life in the name of CHRIST.

Many times the LORD GOD said to Moses "Be strong and courageous". And to Joshua, He said the same thing. It takes courage to stand up in the things of the LORD. It takes courage to walk the walk that Enoch walked. To walk in the footsteps of the giants of faith like Abraham, Elijah, David, etc. it takes a strong character molded by the mighty Spirit of GOD. In the name of the LORD, we shall trust and do valiant things.

Marriages, jobs, families, and finances are destroyed by this kingdom. Water spirits are the cruelest creatures since most of them feed on sexual intercourse. And they harass their victim in their dreams. I had this problem for many years. Different things can cause these spirits to manifest themselves unto you.

Some reasons may be; through idol worship, cultural practices, ancestral worship, pornography, masturbation, having sexual intercourse with a marine agent, through witchcraft, through family initiation, swimming in the water, and others.

When you have opened doors in your life, it is easy for demons to enter and build strongholds. Marine spirits will make your life a living hell if you are not delivered. And it takes an intense deliverance process to cut ties with the powers of the water. It is because of their monitoring powers. They have advanced technology that can see you wherever you go. The house I was living in was plated with demonic spiritual cameras. It is through and by the spiritual eyes opened that I was able to see this.

And the dangerous part about this kingdom is that it will feed you with dreams from their kingdom that if you do not have the spirit of discerning, you will end up following those demonic dreams. Fasting and prayer have to be on your number one list when you are about to embark on deliverance. Spirit never gives up. They are always looking for an opportunity, or an open door to enter.

It is easier for prophets to minister deliverance in this area because prophets can peek into the spirit and see the worldview of the spirit. apart from that, it is an anointing that breaks the yoke.

For me, my life was stagnant. I went to varsity to study BA in film production and media—though spent more than 5 years jobless. To the point where I even gave up on the idea of job seeking. I do want to brag, but I matriculated with fly colors. In school, I was doing really well.

But I always wondered, while at the University of Johannesburg, I found myself spending most of my time reading and studying about religion, especially Christian books of the earlier sages and saints, I was moved and inspired. Mind you, I had pile of television and media communication assignments. But I was always drawn to the Person of GOD, JESUS CHRIST, and the HOLY SPIRIT!

I never thought that one day, I would be a Christian author and a writer. However, before that, I wrote for a certain magazine, poetry, and music. Through music study of the bible and good Christian books, faith was stirred in me, and from that time onwards, the name of the LORD has always been in my mouth. Shift started.

All kinds of prayers are necessary when in trouble. In the name of the LORD, we shall do greater things. I know many who have sleepless nights because of the night demons that feed on sex—sleeping with men and women in dreams.

Call upon the name of the Lord, you shall be saved. At the end of the book, I always leave relevant scriptural prayers for dealing with the satanic powers of the water. The greatest weapon starts with repentance. After that, we can enter into his court with praise and thanksgiving. There are numerous weapons of spiritual warfare and deliverance. Through experience, I have found praise and worship as the powerhouse of deliverance. Of course, you can do all these while praying and fasting.

Ephesians 6:10 Finally, my brethren, be strong in the Lord, and in the power of his might.

The principle is to pray with all kinds of prayers.

Ephesians 6:18 Praying always with all prayer and supplication in the Spirit, and watching thereunto with all perseverance and supplication for all saints;

All kinds of prayers include nothing less than praise, thanksgiving, worship, fasting, giving, supplication, weeping, warfare prayers, silent prayers, prayer walks, proclamations, decrees and declarations, prophetic dancing, and more.

There is a deliverance in the house of God. Total deliverance is a journey.

Authority in the LORD

Your authority rests in the LORD. To know our authority as a child of GOD, you have to know who you are in CHRIST. The Word of the LORD should be your portion and your daily meal.

Psalm 16:5 The LORD is the portion of mine inheritance and of my cup: thou

maintainest my lot.

We are to meditate in the Word day and night. And that is where our success comes from. There is success that comes through meditation. Some breakthroughs you get by positioning yourself at the right time at the right place. While some are just for following biblical principles.

Joshua 1:8 This book of the law shall not depart out of thy mouth; but thou shalt

meditate therein day and night, that thou mayest observe to do according to all

that is written therein: for then thou shalt make thy way prosperous, and then

thou shalt have good success.

Authority in the LORD means you are an expert or specialist when it comes to dividing the scriptures, you walk in the power of the Holy Spirit endowed upon you and diligently observe to do according to the will of GOD.

Believers who walk in authority fear the LORD. The fear of the LORD is the beginning of all wisdom. Again, believers who walk in authority yield to the Holy Spirit—listen intently to the voice of the Spirit of GOD for when to move, and when not to.

This happens when we daily kill the man of flesh—allowing the mighty Spirit of GOD to lead in all things.

The way of prosperity and the way of success comes when the law of GOD departs not in your mouth. The power of life and death is in the tongue. There is life in the tongue when your tongue is filled with wondrous things out of the law of GOD.

Psalm 12:6 The words of the LORD are pure words: as silver tried in a furnace of

earth, purified seven times.

Psalm 19:8-11 The statutes of the LORD are right, rejoicing the heart: the commandment

of the LORD is pure, enlightening the eyes.

9 The fear of the LORD is clean, enduring for ever: the judgments of the

LORD are true and righteous altogether.

10 More to be desired are they than gold, yea, than much fine gold: sweeter

also than honey and the honeycomb.

11 Moreover by them is thy servant warned: and in keeping of them there is

great reward.

In the corporate world, you qualify for a position based on your expertise, qualifications, and experience. Then you assume authority based on the position you have. In the kingdom of GOD you do not qualify for anything, it is granted through mercy and grace. Free gifts out of the free will of GOD. This is amazing!

You can even go deeper in your authority by ingesting the Word, chewing the Word, allow the Word to be the meal of your everyday life. Great in faith is great in the Word. Faith comes by hearing the Word.

Psalms scripture that I just showed you above, expresses that David was the man of Word. He magnified the Word. And GOD magnified him. Being the man after GOD's heart meant that he would do what the LORD says and allow the Holy Spirit to direct his motive. And at the end, gives all glory unto GOD, not to himself. Many fail in this instance, as they want to reserve all glory unto them.

It is David who wrote, "*Psalm 21:13 Be thou exalted, LORD, in thine own strength: so will we sing and praise thy power*".

The king did not want to end up like King Saul. You can hear in his prayer in Psalm 51 saying *"Cast me not away from thy presence; and take not thy holy spirit from Me"* (Psalm 51:10).

The presence of the LORD desperately left King Saul. Rebellion is the number one sin that led him away from the righteous path of the LORD. So, David was conscious of that. He did not want to be the next insane king when the Holy Spirit left.

He was the man after God's own heart because he knew the way to the heart of GOD, which is a contrite and broken spirit.

Psalm 51:17 The sacrifices of God are a broken spirit: a broken and a contrite heart, O
God, thou wilt not despise.

This is the principle to live by. We all make mistakes but at the end of the day humble spirit is what keeps us. Judah was given the responsibility and authority to lead his brethren because of his forgiving spirit. Remember, it was Ruben the firstborn who was to lead his brothers. The LORD went on through the brothers till he found one suitable for spiritual leadership and responsibility.

At some point, the tribe of Ephraim (Joseph) was at the peak of ruling Israel, but the spirit of rebellion tiptoed in, and their leadership was rejected.

It goes to say that while we are given authority by the LORD, we are responsible for maintaining that authority. It's like a car, it has to be maintained continuously for longevity. Likewise, our character must at all times display the spirit that was in CHRIST. All should be done to the greater glory of the MOST HIGH.

The ancient ways to the presence of GOD was through Holiness and righteousness. And yes, faith was the center of it all. With my generation, we are witnessing a falling off in the fear of the LORD. It's the age of grace. Let's not get it confused here folks, grace amplifies holiness and righteousness.

Even a single word from the law of Moses would not be erased. It's because CHRIST came with a grace that abounds more. It all comes from the Law of Moses. And that is *"Love thy neighbor is you love yourself"* and *"And thou shalt love the LORD thy God with all thine heart, and with all thy soul, and with all thy might"*.

Most of us when we talk about power will mention the gifting of the Holy Spirit. There was a man named John the Baptist who worked no miracle but was seen as the great prophet of his generation. He was seen as greater than Moses, Abraham, David, Samuel, etc. It was spoken of him as "Among those born of women there was no one greater than John".

His power was seen in his character. In his preaching. And in his humility. The world will see you as a weak man when you display humility but heaven sees a man beloved. It also goes to say "Humble thyself you shall be lifted".

In the next chapter, I am going to talk about the power works. Here it is clear that authority is vested in individuals who are willing to go the extra mile with their GOD. Shadrack, Meshach, and Abednego were willing to die for their GOD. This is the kind of faith that would not be ignored. Looking also at the life of prophet Elijah, it is a testament to the life of faith. CHRIST himself, the man zealous about the kingdom business of GOD.

Psalm 69:9 For the zeal of thine house hath eaten me up; and the reproaches of them
that reproached thee are fallen upon me.
John 4:34 Jesus saith unto them, My meat is to do the will of him that sent me, and
to finish his work.

Great saints of the bible earned GOD's favor through their dedication and determination through their work. Elijah, Samuel, John the Baptist, Abraham, David, etc. were all about the kingdom of GOD. They saw ahead of time what lies and pressed on to the final destination.

Hebrews 11:1 Now faith is the substance of things hoped for, the evidence of things not
seen.
2 For by it the elders obtained a good report.
By faith Abraham, when he was called to go out into a place which he
should after receive for an inheritance, obeyed; and he went out, not knowing
whither he went.

9 By faith he sojourned in the land of promise, as in a strange country,
dwelling in tabernacles with Isaac and Jacob, the heirs with him of the same
promise:
10 For he looked for a city which hath foundations, whose builder and
maker is God.

Abraham looked for a city which hath foundation, whose builder is ALMIGHTY GOD! It comes to a point in your faith life where you see yourself as a stranger and sojourner in the land when your heart is zealous for the LORD and his house. Even in the midst of wealth, a man like David still woke up in the middle of the night to offer praise and thanksgiving. Let nothing take your eyes away from the things that matter the most. GOD matter!

Authority and power are maintained through your knees. Already believers have authority and power, whether you exercise it or not, you have it. You are anointed and filled with the holy ghost to bear witness to the gospel of CHRIST to the world. The powers of darkness need the power force of GOD to be demolished.

Marine Kingdom.

Here we are going to get deep about this kingdom and how to go about to be free in the LORD. These powers have been hidden in the background yet pulling evil strings upon individuals—harassing, destroying, stealing, and killing. This is the mandate of the Devil.

"The thief comes only to steal and kill and destroy; I have come that they may have life, and have it to the full" (John 10:10).

I wrote a personal testimony about how I was initiated into the dark side by my then-spiritual father without my knowledge. I will visit strange places—see strange kingdoms and the dimension of the activities happening there. When someone who has authority over who's in cult leading you, that demonic anointing becomes your covering. It is so difficult for this individual to leave the cult because of the spirit involved.

I am writing what I know and what I have seen. Deliverance comes from the LORD. The LORD has been with me in those times my spirit was forcefully leaving my body to these strange places. To the marine kingdom, you are recruited. Someone who is already a member has to recruit you, knowingly or unknowingly.

There are seats of authority underwater. The most prominent seats next to Satan are Politicians, religious leaders, business moguls, scientists, doctors, and celebrities. The list is not a closed call. People who have a large following are recruited for deception. It is all about mass deception and mind control.

I have met celebrities, religious leaders, politicians, and the business world in the marine kingdom. All spheres of influence at most are present in these demonic kingdoms. We should be cautious about the food we eat, the clothes we wear, and the media we consume because 90% of them are insinuated by the devil himself.

Most of us are unaware of this. We should once again go back to the basis of singing songs about the blood of Jesus and plead for the blood of Jesus at our homes, churches, workplaces, and schools. We are at the brink where it is survival of the fittest. It is like in the jungle where anyone can be a victim.

These days, even social media influencers are targeted because of the amass followers they have, so to spread satanic agendas. All sectors are governed underwater since men made a pact with demonic forces of the water realm. I am someone who used to drink water from the rivers since I come from a village called Mashashane, in South Africa.

I woke up to a shock one evening when I received a revelation from the river I had drawn water from. Mermaids or mermen aren't what they show you on television or in movies. They are not as beautiful and innocent as you think. They are the fallen ones, and their beauty has been stripped from them, however, they can also manifest in anyhow and masquerade beauty.

I saw an ancient old rugged-looking being with hair falling. I can even still see that picture in my mind now. They look scary and intimidating. But what you see in the marine kingdom is a beauty in disguise. Their cities, towns, libraries, roads, etc. everything is fine and out of this world. It is a strange dimension since it is all happening under the sea.

At one point there was a meeting, Satan, was there. There were seats of politicians, religious leaders, musicians, etc. and they were talking about the ongoing discussion—the new world order. So sad that almost every president of every country is part of this demonic group.

While the MOST HIGH rewards you for righteousness, Satan rewards you for wickedness. I thank GOD that earlier on, I knew about this kingdom. Sometimes the spirit of GOD will lift me and go to that kingdom and see what they are doing, for me to pray strategically. Christians are to wage spiritual warfare the right way. As I always say, you cannot win the battle you don't know, or defeat the enemy you don't know. Joshua sent spies to survey the land before he conquered it. The principle Is still the same, you gather information, study, and spy on your opponent before engaging in war.

As a strategic deliverance minister, you have to be aware of the spiritual warfare that is in the land, the water, and the air. These spirits you cannot see with your naked eye but with the eyes of your mind. GOD shows you dreams and visions at night about these spirits and their agenda.

Ephesians 6:12 For we wrestle not against flesh and blood, but against principalities,
against powers, against the rulers of the darkness of this world, against spiritual
wickedness in high places.

Here Paul is talking about the powers of the air. Satan is the prince of the power of the air. Indeed, the god of this world. If you want to see the Devil as the god of this world, look at the leaders of your countries, and observe whom they are serving by their fruits. Behind every power and authority, there is spirit. if the spirit is not the Holy Ghost, then it is of the Devil. The spirit of CHRIST brings liberty. I doubt there is any liberty in your country, therefore, we have to stand up and call upon the LORD.

Most people don't recognize that there is a spiritual Marine Kingdom in the ocean. The Bible talks about Leviathan as the sea serpent, the strongest of the sea, unkillable and uncatchable! Or in myths and legends such as the Kraken, as we see in movies today.

But the Marine kingdom is alive and the strongest among all the demonic kingdoms in land, sea, and air. At creation, when Earth was without form, it was covered with water, one of the first key elements in creation, and also in our lives today, as we are made up of 70% water! And this is where they have created a kingdom where divine strategies are planned and executed.

You divided the sea by your might; you broke the heads of the sea monsters on the waters [Psalm 74:13]

These Spirits are not friendly, they are demonic forces in the waters who aim to rule and control their region, and its people, with anger, violence, and madness! We might remember the story in the Bible about the madman who was tormented by demons from the marine kingdom, and when faced with Jesus they asked to be cast out in the pigs, which ran and drowned in the sea to return to where they came from!

Marine spirits are responsible for many things such as violence, madness, anger, cultism, lust, and sexual perversion, for being single and unable to get a partner [chronic spinster/bachelorhood], divorce, bankruptcy, sex dreams/or having sex in your dreams, by becoming a spirit husband or wife. Also, things that are dead in our lives; dead organs, dead womb, brain, or dead spiritual life all come from the bottom of the sea [Job 26:5, Psalm 104, Micah 7:19].

So, how does the marine kingdom gain entrance into people's live?

1. Dedication at birth, or even adulthood

2. Coming down the line of your ancestors

3. Allowing them to enter your body or property [possession]

4. Sexual intercourse

5. Borrowing/Buying items from people that were committed to these spirits

Signs that you are initiated into the Marine kingdom:

✓ Barrenness Sometimes Is Associated with It.

✓ Chronic Masturbation.

✓ Dreams of Swimming in Rivers or Oceans.

✓ Dreams of Having Sex with known or unknown people are connected to Marine spirits.

✓ Dream of Playing with snakes and the presence of frogs in one's dream.

✓ Sudden and Mysterious missing of personal effects like Undergarments.

✓ Excessive Pride – Uncontrollable Anger And Outbursts.

✓ Suicidal Thoughts And Dreams of Being killed.

✓ Fear of Water, i.e. rivers, lakes, oceans.

✓ Constant Irritating Smell Even After Bathing.

✓ Wearing of Ornaments From Unknown Sources.

✓ Getting Mysterious Objects At Your House, Room, Or Even Mysterious Letters.

✓ Been Initiated Through Unholy Sex, Fornication, or Sex with Agents.

✓ Bedwetting Is Clear And Also Associated With the Spirit Of Immaturity and Stagnation.

✓ Chronic Spinsterhood And Chronic Bachelorhood.

✓ Excessive Urge For Sex Without Control.

✓ Excessive Lust.

✓ Dreams Of Receiving Money From A Very Beautiful Woman Or Man.

✓ Breaking Of Other People's Marriage And Be Without Remorse.

✓ A Youthful Man or Woman, Unmarried And Yet Desires Married Men or Women.

✓ Marine Kingdom is the Number one Promoter Of Polygamy.

✓ Addicted to Music Ungodly Music.

✓ Dreams Of Being Given Excess Wealth from Unknown Sources In Return of Favors.

Ways to deal with the Marine Kingdom:

1. Accept Jesus as your Lord and Savior

2. Engaging in Spiritual Warfare prayers to remove these spirits

3. Confession, repentance, and denouncing dedication

4. Be rooted and grounded in the Word of God [the Bible]

5. Praying in tongues and commanding these spirits to release you

You must engage in spiritual warfare prayers against marine spirits to break all the strongholds of these demons in your life in Jesus' name, otherwise, they will continue hurting and controlling your life! But greater is He in you that can remove these spirits, but just like Jesus who told the spirits to "go" out of the madman, so must you!

Spiritual warfare and deliverance.

If we are going to the promised land of rest, some things are bound to hinder us from reaching that place. So, spiritual warfare will be part of the game. The new generation of Joshua after the death of Moses, the man of GOD, had to arm themselves for war to be able to conquer territory.

We conquer territory in the spirit world before it manifests physically. Take an example from witches and wizards, they spend sleepless nights in their coven meetings strategizing how they are going to destroy you. And in these meetings, they go in spirit—Astra projecting. 80 % of what they do, they do it in spirit. As a child of the MOST HIGH, if you aren't mature spiritually, they will weaken you, and eventually destroy your destiny.

Spiritual warfare is a must for every believer in CHRIST. The heavenly places are filled with millions of dark spirits that are eager to torment any part of your life if you allow them to. From time to time, we ought to do spiritual checkups and introspection to see if we are still on the path of light.

Personally, through the grace and diligent study of the Word, I have taught myself self-deliverance. Self-deliverance is as powerful as deliverance from the minister if you believe. At the end of the day, the just shall be justified through faith. Faith is what matters. Faith is taking the next step. It is an action. The MOST HIGH GOD rewards faith.

Hebrews 11:22-23 Let us draw near with a true heart in full assurance of faith, having our

hearts sprinkled from an evil conscience, and our bodies washed with pure
water.
23 Let us hold fast the profession of our faith without wavering;
(for he is
faithful that promised;)

Faith is an issue of the heart. When it talks about the eyes of your understanding, it is the Holy Spirit. the measure of faith in your heart determines how far can you go with the LORD. He has blessed you with the gift of faith to change the situation in your life. When dealing with demonic powers, it is not by mighty but by the Spirit of the LIVING GOD. So, faith overcomes the world. Meaning, that faith overcomes the Devil who is the god of this world. Against, he is the prince of the power of the air.

The heavenly place that Paul talked about in Ephesians is the kingdom of the air. The unseen realm is powered by principalities and powers of darkness who are against territories, kingdoms, countries, cities, towns, etc. One principality can rule the whole country, but assign another strongman to provinces, towns, cities, and villages.

I know some believers disagree about the second heaven theory. The secret of the LORD are will those who fear his name. The Holy Spirit continues to reveal to us things we would not know with our minds. The spirit world is so vast. And there is a lot that is happening, that, if GOD can open your eyes to see the spirit world, I swear you would ask the LORD to take back his gift. Especially if he can deal with you in the demonic realm. If he can show you the kingdom of darkness.

That is why Prophets are misunderstood in this world. And this stigma has long been around since ancient times. Prophets are loners. So to sharpen that ear to hear the sound of the spirit. and to hear the small still voice of the Holy Spirit. usually, it is in a lonely time when you hear the voice of the LORD. The spirit of the LORD brings liberty and peace.

Let's talk about the air realm. There is the first heaven, the second heaven, and the third heaven. The disembodied spirits are the evil spirits of the Nephilim destroyed during the floods of Noah. Lucifer also fell with millions of angels. Apart from Lucifer, 200 watchers had sex with women—recorded in the book of Enoch and Genesis 6. The evil spirits hover around in the sky, looking for a way in a man. The sin of man gives this spirit legal authority to enter man's body.

It is to say, above our homes, in the air, there a thousands of evil spirits. Above the peak of the mountain, in the space of the clouds, there is a strongman who gives orders to these demons. Strongman are serious powers of authority. There are levels of degrees in the demonic. JESUS CHRIST granted us the power to cast out demons and also to bind strongmen.

The first heaven is where the powers of authority seats. They control what is going on in a region. But they have control only where they have legal rights. Satan can only control where there is a legal right to do so. He is limited.

The second heaven is his domain—headquarters. Where there are dangerous spirits like the queen of heaven, Ashtoreth, Jezebel, etc. this is the kingdom like any other kingdom. This is where the souls of men and women are caged. The real battle of spiritual warfare is here but with the angelic beings. This is where Angel Michael fought the Prince of Persia for the release of Gabriel to bring Daniel's message.

Principalities mostly name themselves according to the city of the domain they rule. If there is a principality in Johannesburg, he would call himself the prince of Johannesburg. However, these are fallen angels. You cannot cast them out. They are not demons but fallen angels. You can only restrict their assignment. You can be like Daniel and intercede for the dispatcher of angelic powers like Michael to fight for you when dealing with serious powers.

If you can picture yourself seated in the heavenly places with CHRIST, your faith will explode. Your level of spiritual perception will change. You start seeing yourself as above principalities and powers of darkness as you are seated in the seat of authority with CHRIST who has triumphed.

Colossians 1:15 Who is the image of the invisible God, the firstborn of every creature:
16 For by him were all things created, that are in heaven, and that are in
earth, visible and invisible, whether they be thrones, or dominions, or
principalities, or powers: all things were created by him, and for him: 17 And he
is before all things, and by him all things consist.

We are dealing with the invisible kingdoms that are pulling strings in the background. The naked eye cannot see spirits. Through the eyes of your mind—the Holy Spirit, you can see beyond time and space. This few months I have been researching and writing about the discerning spirit (Spirit of discernment). This gift is important especially when dealing with spiritual attacks from the realm of darkness. It comes with words of wisdom, knowledge, and understanding of the spirit world.

Many times my life has been spared through this gift. And many has ago, I had a personal encounter with the LORD, and He was telling me about "intuition". Sometimes you will not get the word for a specific thing, or rather prophecy for a season when you need it most, if you can follow your intuition—your spirit within, you will succeed because the Holy Spirit is intertwined with our spirit, and bear witness to your heart.

This is also important when you are dealing with the marine powers. You will need the word for the moment. Your dream and vision life has to be covered by the power of the BLOOD OF JESUS. Marine powers through dream and vision. Sometimes they will confuse your life. Cover everything with the blood of the Cross. The power of GOD shall be revealed. Sing Holy Spirit-inspired songs—especially about the power of the BLOOD OF CHRIST.

Ephesians 1:19 And what is the exceeding greatness of his power to us-ward who
believe, according to the working of his mighty power,
20 Which he wrought in Christ, when he raised him from the dead, and set
him at his own right hand in the heavenly places,

Every believer in the Cross is seated in the heavenly places with CHRIST. CHRIST's priesthood is different from others, His priesthood is eternal. This means that you have been with CHRIST all along before you were even created, spiritually. The kingdom of GOD is spiritual. GOD is spiritual. JESUS CHRIST is a spirit being. However, He came in the bodily form for our redemption. The redemption plan of GOD has been ever since before creation. GOD knows the end from the beginning. Knows the thoughts of a man from afar.

In spirit, you are crafted in CHRIST who overcame. And that makes you an overcomer! Even though darkness has its way around us, we are the light of this world through CHRIST. Stir up your light! Arise and shine!

Ephesians 1:21 Far above all principality, and power, and might, and dominion, and

every name that is named, not only in this world, but also in that which is to

come:

In the world to come CHRIST is still the KINGS! The wisdom of this world would try to convince you that Satan does not exist; it is all in your mind. The people in high power are those blinding many to believe the fallacy. Our enemy, the Devil sits at the seat of high authority in this world—manipulating, controlling, stealing, and killing.

A defeated foe indeed! But the media magnifies him to weaken man's faith. Our gateway through the presence of GOD is the Holy Spirit. the Holy Spirit in you is bigger than Satan a million times. The Holy Spirit is GOD. In other words, GOD resides in you. CHRIST in you is the hope of your glory. CHRIST in you is your salvation. No weapon formed against us shall prosper. It is the truth that shall set people free. In the name of the LORD GOD MOST HIGH be free!

GOD is above culture. GOD is above religion. GOD is above tradition. GOD is above all wisdom, all knowledge, and all understanding. Serve Him only in the name of JESUS CHRIST!

Ephesians 2:6 And hath raised us up together, and made us sit together in heavenly
places in Christ Jesus:

As we are in CHRIST, we have all the spiritual blessings to free ourselves and our brethren from spiritual bondage of all kinds. The Psalmist says we are a little lower than the angels. This is great authority indeed. What's more? Psalm 82:6 *"Ye are gods"*. We all come from the HOLY ONE!

Psalm 82:6 I have said, Ye are gods; and all of you are children of the most High.

In dealing with the demonic realm like the marine kingdom, a very basic strategy of success in war is to know one's enemy. Without exception, a general would never take his army against another army without first preparing the soldiers.

Foundational to that preparation would be a study of the strengths and weaknesses of the enemy. Failure to study the enemy would virtually guarantee defeat— even if the opposing army were inferior. Throughout this book, I talk in depth about who our enemy is, you will be surprised that even though this book is about the marine battle, most focus is on the Devil himself and overcoming strategies of victory against his tricks.

Most of my writing is in light of spiritual warfare and prayer mainly because we are in war. The battle is for the LORD but He uses us as His mighty army to dismantle the powers of darkness throughout the world. People must be free from demonic entanglement. There is freedom in the LORD.

CHRIST has to be known from sun rising to sun down. This is the greatest commission of the gospel.

Psalm 34: 8 O taste and see that the LORD is good: blessed is the man that trusteth in him.

him.

✦ *Affirm your faith in Christ*

Wherefore, holy brethren, partakers of the heavenly calling, consider the Apostle and High Priest of our profession, Christ Jesus— Heb 3:1

Now faith is the substance of things hoped for, the evidence of things not seen- Hebrews 11:6

Lately many have been doing affirmations. It has been found that when you speak positivity into your life—the outlook will breed positivity. It has also been noted that positive thinking equates positive life. Well, here we have something valuable—being in Christ!

Ephesians 2:6 And hath raised up together, and made us sit together in heavenly places in Christ

The benefit of being in Christ is that you are above all principalities, powers, and thrones of the darkness. You trample upon the young lions and adders (Psalm 91:10). You behold the face of God and transform from glory to glory. When you are in Christ, you have overcome. It is the essence of faith that guarantees the benefits and features of being in the house of the LIVING GOD.

The road to redemption requires your affirmation in Christ. You believe, therefore, you speak. You will learn that you are so much more in Christ "ye are gods". You are more than the precious things we seek of this world. *You are blessed of the Lord that made the heavens and earth (Psalm 115:15).*

It takes nothing more than your heart to accept the Lord to be your savior. *Know ye that the Lord he is God: it is he that hath made us, and not we ourselves; we are his people, and the sheep of his pasture Psalm 100:3). Create in me a clean heart, O God, and renew a right spirit in me (Psalm 53:10).*

Before we proceed in self-deliverance, you have to ensure that you are in Christ. As a Christian community, we use Roman 10:9 *"that if thou shalt confess with thy mouth the Lord Jesus, and shalt believe in thine heart that God hath raised him from the dead, thou shalt be saved"*

"For with the heart man believeth unto righteousness; and with thy mouth confession is made unto salvation"

You cannot heal what you cannot confess. Most of the challenges we conquer, it is because we confess to salvation. Faith is seeing the positive side of the ugly things. When things go rough—amid the roughness you see precious diamonds. We overcome not only by the blood of the lamb but by also our word of testimony—and also not loving our lives unto death.

I like the woman Deborah, prophetess, leader, and judge of Israel. We only have two chapters in The Judges dedicated to this woman—but her faith was immensely on the rock. She will compose songs of victory for Israel before even they go to the battlefield. That's pure faith, my friend. You celebrate the goodness of the Lord before you see His strong hand. This is what we can also learn from the life of King David—the sweet psalmist of Israel.

The life of a believer isn't a walk in the park. It is also not glamorous some claim it to be. You can be lost if you can listen to certain pastors—especially those who dwell much on the prosperity gospel. The best decision to make is to study the bible yourself. Immerse deeply in it. You can walk in authority and power in the area of your knowledge. Knowledge is power.

Affirming your faith in God is paramount to your walk with God. you can make affirmations through confessions, declarations, decrees, etc. Don't be like the sons of Sceva who ministered deliverance without authority in Christ. Be straight with Christ. It is through Him and by Him that all things are subdued under our feet. The Devil is under our feet because of what He did on the Cross. The power is in the blood of the Lamb (Revelation 12:11).

Humble yourself

• God Almighty chooses to humble Himself and be involved in our humanity (personal lives). (See Psalm 113:5–6.)

• God chooses to use ordinary people to achieve His magnificent plans and bring Himself glory. (See I Corinthians 1:25–31.)

• Although a member of the Trinity and deserving of glory, Jesus deflected praise to the Father. (See John 17:3–4.)

• Jesus humbled Himself to be obedient to God's plan by becoming a man, dwelling on earth, and even dying on a cross. (See Philippians 2:6–8.)

• The Holy Spirit prods our hearts, wanting us to humble ourselves before God. It is our choice to be humble or remain prideful. (See Acts 7:51.)

2 Chronicles 33:12-16

12 And when he was in affliction, he besought the LORD his God, and humbled himself greatly before the God of his fathers, 13 And prayed unto him: and he was intreated of him, and heard his supplication, and brought him again to Jerusalem into his kingdom. Then Manasseh knew that the LORD he was God. 14 Now after this he built a wall without the city of David, on the west side of Gihon, in the valley, even to the entering in at the fish gate, and compassed about Ophel, and raised it up a very great height, and put captains of war in all the fenced cities of Judah. 15 And he took away the strange gods, and the idol out of the house of the LORD, and all the altars that he had built in the mount of the house of the LORD, and in Jerusalem, and cast them out of the city. 16 And he repaired the altar of the LORD, and sacrificed thereon peace offerings and thank offerings, and commanded Judah to serve the LORD God of Israel.

The act of humility is not small to God. It doesn't matter how many sins you have committed. God values a humble spirit. King Manasseh was evil and influenced also the nation to serve other gods. God will visit you countless times because he cares about our souls. He doesn't want your soul wandering. In the house of the Living God, there are mansions. He is the restorer of souls if we can come before his presence in humility.

A humble soul He will not rebuke. Moses was the meekest person on the earth. God revealed Himself mightily through him because of his humility. Being humble is putting God first. Allowing Him to be the leader of our lives while we trust the process. It is not about respecting people. Humility is about God. There are so many people across cultures who are respectful to elders and other people. Respect is a good gesture of morality—but humility is more than that. The way of humility according to the bible is less of me, and more of God. He must increase and I must decrease. This is the reason why John the Baptist was counted worthy more than the prophets who have been before him. He counted all unworthy than what he carried. This is the spirit we require—a selfless spirit to serve the Living God.

When you are afflicted, seek the Lord. David says I will praise the Lord at all times. When you are afflicted, remember the Lord. He doesn't pinpoint fingers of the wrong things you have done as some of us do. When you seek Him will all your heart—He will be right there to pull you through. The Bible says the truth shall set you free. When we can acknowledge that we have derailed, we can also acknowledge our shortfalls before Him. Humble yourself, He will lift you.

"Yea, all of you be subject one to another, and be clothed with humility: for God resisteth the proud, and giveth grace to the humble. Humble yourselves therefore under the mighty hand of God, that he may exalt you in due time." I Peter 5:5, 6. The word humble in the latter verse signifies to make self-low.

In Proverbs 6:3 the word has yet a deeper signification, which is to trample on self. Taking these two texts we have a very important thought before us. It suggests to our minds the proper and scriptural position of self. Many other references to Scripture could be added but these, I believe, are sufficient.

Our every attitude toward God must be in this utmost submission; always ready and willing to glorify Him without the least desire for any glory to ourselves; always seeking to represent Him to this world without the least desire of self-representation: always seeking, as Jesus did, "not mine own will but the will of Him that sent me." Like the branch laden with the delicious fruit of the vine, it is never spoken of for the good fruit borne, but the vine receives the praise. So we are to be so meekly and humbly the branches to bear the precious fruit of Christ— always to honor Him in every step, willing to be hidden away out of sight so that He may always be manifest.

Confess any known sin
— 1 John 1:9

Repentance is the key to a victorious life. Many don't realize that it is a weapon of warfare. Demons lose legal rights when they repent. Create in me a clean heart is the song of repentance. God Almighty brings a clean slate unto you when you humble yourself by confessing your sins.

Psalm 32:5 I acknowledged my sin unto thee, and mine iniquity have I not hid. I said, I will confess my transgressions unto the LORD; and thou forgavest the iniquity of my sin. Selah.

You cannot succeed by hiding your iniquity. It eats you more when you sin. The guilty conscious of your sin will eat you up till you see the need to come clean. O Lord create in me a clean heart.

You confess any sin you know of. Dreams you see at night say a lot about your walk with God. Take note of your dream. The majority of it may be soulish dreams but a believer's walk of life must be filled with prophetic dreams. During sleep hours most of the times, God reveals things pertaining to our lives. You may also trace your track record of your lineage through dreams. Yes, God can show you if you ask Him.

Repent of all sins
— Prov. 28:3

Repentance means a change of mind. You cannot be making the same mistake again and again—repenting for the same mistake now and then. John the Baptist baptized people once and for all. I am not saying we aren't going to backslide, but we should allow God to quicken our spirit. Allowing the Holy Spirit to take the lead in our daily lives.

You carry the cross 24/7. God is faithful—He will always strengthen our spirits. God is spirit. He deals with us spiritually. You confess and repent all the sins committed. Also, the sins of our forefathers because punishments for their sins affect our spiritual maturity. You cannot experience the presence of the Almighty to the fullest with a load of garbage that is still connected to you spiritually. The devil uses this kind of entry-level of ancestral curses to wreck our lives havoc. I am from a place where the practice of witchcraft is so BIG!

The majority of family members certified as believers venerate ancestral spirits. This creates a doorway to idolization. You see them as meditators between you and God. This is the stand of most African-initiated churches. Someone who is fully committed to serving the Living God is seen as a sell-out and also as a disobedient child before his or her ancestral lineage. The thing is that if your ancestors worshipped the sun, moon, or stars, the demons behind these things will take over your life. It is the spirit of transference. Whereby you allow the things of your ancestors to take the lead as they did before you.

Forgive all other people
— Matt. 18:23–25

Forgiveness is a medicine to our hearts. It benefits the one who is hurting, harboring deep grudges. When you don't forgive your own heart condemns you. Freedom is when you let it go. When you free yourself from things that aren't bringing the light into your life. It is a command from the Lord for us to forgive each other because mistakes are relatable. We still going to wrong each other until the end of age. What holds us together is the spirit of humility and forgiveness more than anything.

Self-deliverance results in success when you acknowledge, confess, and repent your sin. Forgiveness to yourself and others is a doorway to freedom. Free your heart from the load of pain by being the bigger person even if you did nothing wrong. The main reason why we do not forgive each other is because we weigh how much someone has hurt us. If the weight is heavy slack off. I also believe in the phrase "time heals". It also heals fast if we are to let it go.

Legal rights of demons.

There has to be a bargain for demons to be within a person. Note that, the Devil is a legalist but God is the judge of them all. The Devil does not do as he pleases—he gets permission from God. when you sin, you give him enough chance to bargain for your life. The result of sin is death.

We should learn to think of Satan as a lawyer demanding his rights before God. Learn to think of JESUS CHRIST as an advocate, a lawyer, defending our rights before God. The perfect example is to look at the life of Job—he was accused and persecuted for being righteous. We all know the pattern of the devil; to steal, kill, and destroy. You are only the devil's favorite when you do what he does—destroying souls. He uses demons to get through us.

If we take away their legal rights before God to be in a human body, then we can cast them out relatively easily. This method takes away much of the violence that is exhibited when the demons have a right to remain. We had violence and strong manifestations before God taught us this lesson.

We would have to hold people on the floor to keep them from hurting themselves and others. We have even had the demons tell us that they would like to leave but they couldn't because the person had unforgiveness, they were cursed, or for some other reason. Once a demon told us that he was held in by a curse.

The following are some general categories of demons' legal rights that you need to remove before you start casting out: soul ties, false religions, occult activities, cursed objects, sins of ancestors, and curses. You need to deal with any sin that has been committed that may have opened the door for demons to come in, especially unforgiveness. God taught us that unforgiveness is the most important part of DELIVERANCE.

Break with occult, false religion, secret societies

So much unfortunate that is happening especially in the body of Christ lately, is the result of untruthfulness. I have observed that if you want to be safe and on the right path, follow God not men. We all know that God anoints men into offices, but that shouldn't shift you from God. Most men of God like to act as demigods or junior gods to their congregation.

Anything that drives us away from God—it is an idol. God forbid. Our forefathers have served nature or anything they could see, that's why we struggling with generational curses in our lives. For me personally, I have struggled a lot with ancestral curses. It is your duty as the warrior of God to see yourself delivered. Salvation belongs to God. We can only draw our strength from the might of God. We are only strong in the Lord, and in the power of His might.

The step to total salvation is renouncing everything in your family line that does not align with God. Breaking with the occult, witchcraft, false religion, secret societies, etc. Demons have to have the legal right to you before they can torment you. Without the legal right, they cannot have access to you. Satan will tempt you to sin so that he can torment you with his legion of demons.

Deuteronomy 18:10-14

There shall not be found among you any one that maketh his son or his daughter to pass through the fire, or that useth divination, or an observer of times, or an enchanter, or a witch. 11 Or a charmer, or a consulter with familiar spirits, or a wizard, or a necromancer. 12 For all that do these things are an abomination unto the LORD: and because of these abominations the LORD thy God doth drive them out from before thee. 13 Thou shalt be perfect with the LORD thy God. 14 For these nations, which thou shalt possess, hearkened unto observers of times, and unto diviners: but as for thee, the LORD thy God hath not suffered thee so to do.

2 Chronicles 33:6

And he caused his children to pass through the fire in the valley of the son of Hinnom: also he observed times, and used enchantments, and used witchcraft, and dealt with a familiar spirit, and with wizards: he wrought much evil in the sight of the LORD, to provoke him to anger.

Isaiah 47:9

But these two things shall come to thee in a moment in one day, the loss of children, and widowhood: they shall come upon thee in their perfection for the multitude of thy sorceries, and for the great abundance of thine enchantments.

You cannot fight what you don't know and expect to win. Life is warfare itself, demons that are derailing your deliverance will want to keep you bound. They don't want you to know that they exist. This is the biggest lie the devil is using right now to keep you ignored and idle when coming to spiritual matters. It is not like the kingdom of the devil is advancing, it is just that many of us are ignorant of the word of God.

Most believers are victims of generational evil stronghold of family matters. This has been me for the most part. I learned the hard way that you can discipline your life in a godly manner but still experience evil backlashes from family alters that you don't even know about. If there has ever been someone in your lineage who practiced witchcraft or all kinds of dark science, you will suffer the effect of these spirits. Spirituality has far much impact on your physical walk. This is the spiritual walk of the warriors of the Living God. God calls us warriors.

✦ *Prepare to be released from every curse*
— *Gal. 3:13–14*

Preparation is important. Expect to be delivered. This is an act of faith, seeing yourself whole and healthy, delivered and protected by the mercy and love of God. Usually, deliverance takes place in the church. We cannot limit God; you will never know the day of your miracle. But expect miracles every day!

Scriptures declare that we are free in Christ. This means that already the enemy is defeated. Principalities and powers of the enemy are under our feet. We go into the battlefield already knowing that we are the victors. This is what Deborah; the prophetess of Israel did. She composed a victory song before the battle. This is a pure act of faith. You see it before it manifests. Apart from that you can fill your heart with all deliverance scriptures. Faith also comes through reading and ingesting the word of God in your heart.

✦ *Take your stand with God*
— *Rom. 8:31*

Take your stand with God like Moses will ask "Who is for God?". In a world full of idolization at the fullest—take a stand for God. Abraham came out of his people—out of idolization. You can come out as well. Men and women of God who stood for God, and with God, made names for themselves. When you are for God, it is even easy for your family to sideline you. But at the end, the glory of God shall shine upon you that it won't be hard for them to notice you. It doesn't matter how much you are worth financially. Lazarus was a very powerful man—but the miracle performed upon his life shocked the whole world. If you are for God and, stand still—the hand of the Living God is upon you man of God— Women of God.

When you stand in God, it means that you are seated with him in the heavenly places (Ephesians 2:6). The doorway is the Living Rock. Moses wanted to see the glory of the Lord so badly, and you know what God covered Moses with? The living rock! No one performed breathtaking miracles like Moses. The angel of God that was behind Moses' miraculous power is Christ Himself. The Old Testament prophets saw Christ beforehand. Even Abraham had an encounter with Christ.

Trust God for your deliverance. Trust God for your whole life. Surrender your life fully unto God. The upright shall at all times be blessed. And shall also inherit the earth. The earth and everything in it belong to the Lord— The king of the Glory.

✦ *Expel – Release self!*

Christians can cast out demons of any rank in the Mighty Name of JESUS CHRIST (Mark 16:17; Luke 10:17-20). However, some situations require more experience than the ordinary Christian would have. These situations are where ordinary DELIVERANCE has not done the job. Here an experienced DELIVERANCE minister is required. Don't be afraid to get involved as the Holy Spirit leads you. There are too many cowardly Christians and Ministers who are afraid to get involved in this DELIVERANCE which is controversial and unpopular.

Expelling demons is as easy as ABC. You command them to leave you. You don't interview or converse with them like some pastors and prophets do. Jesus commanded them to leave people's bodies. In these last days, God has spoken to us with his Son. The indwelling of the holy spirit within our hearts testifies that Yeshua is the messiah. Dreams and visions people all over the world are experiencing are to the ceiling. This season the spirit is revealing so much to the body of Christ.

The satanic tactic of the enemy is coming to the surface. The marine kingdom which was hidden, now every believer is aware of the satanic mission. It is a good thing to know what you are fighting with. Lack of knowledge will keep you in bondage. I have seen this in my life the more I know about a particular subject—the more I walk in authority in that area.

The more you know about spiritual warfare and deliverance, the more you will command and walk in authority. It is the bible that sets us free. You can start by filling your heart and soul with the deliverance scripture. Meditate deeply on them till they are sealed within your heart.

Declaring Basis For Deliverance – God's Word!

Lord Jesus I humbly claim the following scriptures as the basis for deliverance and I speak the written word of Jehovah Yahweh, as well as your words in the New Testament _________and come against the enemy with these 5 scriptures: 1. Matthew 10: 1 - And when He had called His twelve disciples to Him, He gave them power over unclean spirits, to cast them out, and to heal all kinds of sickness and all kinds of disease. 2. Matthew 10: 8 Heal the sick, cleanse the lepers, raise the dead,[a] cast out demons. Freely you have received, freely give. 3. Matthew 18:20 Lord, You said, "Where two or more are gathered together in my name, there I am also in the midst of them."– 4. Matthew 18: 18 "Truly I say to you, whatever you bind on earth shall have been bound in heaven, and whatever you loose on earth shall have been loosed in heaven." 5. Luke 10:19 Behold, I give you the authority to trample on serpents and scorpions, and over all the power of the enemy, and nothing shall by any means hurt you.

DELIVERANCE PRAYER Based on the experience of Derek Prince www.derekprince.org

Jesus Christ, I affirm that You are the Son of God and the only door to eternal life. I acknowledge that You died for my sins on the cross 2000 years ago and rose from the dead by the power of Your Holy Spirit. That same Holy Spirit power is greater than all other powers and has already defeated Satan and his demons on the cross 2000 years ago. Jesus, I renounce all arrogance, self-sufficiency, and pride, which was the downfall of Satin. I have nothing and am nothing, except in You my hiding place. Jesus, I confess all my sins, especially

---

I confess all my omissions, especially ________________________________ I confess the sins of my ancestors, especially ________________________________ Jesus, I apologize for all the sins and omissions which I have just now stated. I promise to try (with Your help and the help of others) not to repeat these sins. If I slip and fall, I will try to confess immediately and turn to You for help. With Your help, I will refuse temptation and negative attitudes, especially rejection. With Your help I will obey my doctor/mate/pastor/employer & not my negative feelings/thoughts. With Your help, I will be the friend that I need/want in my life. With Your help, I will take a shower, brush my teeth, make my bed, do my laundry, & eat fruit. Jesus, Forgive everyone whether they deserve it or not because You forgave me and held nothing back. I now especially forgive ____ Jesus, As you bring to my attention any occult activity, situation, or object that displeases you. I will repent and sever my relationship with it, even if it is very valuable. Jesus, Thank you for becoming a curse on the cross for me, so that I may be freed of all curses that are due to my sins or the sins of my ancestors. Jesus,

I take my stand, in Your name, Jesus, against all Satan's demons. I trust that You will take care of the demons and also take care of me. I resist the devil, in Your name, Jesus. Amen.

Demons, I speak to you that have control over me. IN THE NAME OF JESUS I bind you. IN THE NAME OF JESUS I command you to quietly go from me now under the feet of Jesus. IN THE NAME OF JESUS I expel you. IN THE NAME OF JESUS I command you never to return.

Jesus, I adore and praise you for your deliverance of the demon of ______________________________. Jesus, I adore and praise you for your deliverance of the demon of ______________________________. Jesus, I adore and praise you for your deliverance of the demon of

______________________________. Jesus, I adore and praise you for your deliverance of the demon of ______________________________.

Jesus, I ask You to fill with Your Holy Spirit those empty spots vacated by the demons who left so that when they try to come back there will be no place for them.

Jesus, Bless you, Lord. Thank you, Lord. My heart is full of joy and gratefulness.

Blood of Jesus Prayer.

Blood prayer sets the captives free. The tiny drop of the blood of CHRIST will silence matters in the kingdom of darkness. The is nothing powerful than the blood of JESUS CHRIST. As you are dealing with an ancestral stronghold, curses, marine powers, and a strongman of evil in your life, the blood is potent to set you free in an instant. For me, this came through a revelation. The LORD revealed the power of His blood.

Just by singing blood songs such as "Awesome Blood" and "Nothing but the Blood" you can be delivered from any satanic stronghold. However, it all comes down to faith. You have to believe that what you are praying for shall surely come to pass.

You can cover your home with the blood of JESUS just like Moses who ordered the Israelites in Egypt to put the blood in their doorpost. Whoever did put the blood of the lamb on their doorpost was spared from death. The blood of JESUS delivers you from the grip of death. Death no longer has power over you. Death is a spirit. Death is our enemy. When do not die but sleep in the LORD and rise in the LORD. Heaven is our ultimate home.

The Angel of Death destroyed the firstborn of Egypt, including Pharaoh's son who was about to precede him. A man who has not made a blood covenant with CHRIST will always be in Egypt. Egypt is the house of bondage. The yoke of bondage will be heavy on you. Deliverance comes from the house of the LORD.

Exodus 12:12 For I will pass through the land of Egypt this night, and will smite all the

firstborn in the land of Egypt, both man and beast; and against all the gods of
Egypt I will execute judgment: I am the LORD.
13 And the blood shall be to you for a token upon the houses where
ye are:
and when I see the blood, I will pass over you, and the plague shall
not be upon
you to destroy you, when I smite the land of Egypt.

The blood of Jesus is one of the potent weapons against spiritual wickedness in high places and to demolish every stronghold of satanic forces. It cannot achieve less for you.

Revelation 12:11: *"And they overcame him by the blood of the Lamb and the Word of their testimony and they loved not their lives unto the death."*

The blood of Jesus can never lose its power because it is a divine blood. Jesus is the only begotten of the father" (John 1:14). The blood of Jesus avails for everything imaginable. If we are going to experience the power in the blood of Jesus we have to personally apply it to our lives and our situations. We apply the blood of Jesus, by decrees, *i.e.* we confess it.

The blood of Jesus speaks better things than the blood of Abel" (Hebrews 12:24). The blood of Jesus can speak destruction upon your enemies, healing to your body, protection to your family, *etc.* The blood of Jesus brings life to you. The Bible says, "The life of the flesh is in the blood: . . ."(Leviticus 17:11). The blood of Jesus contains the life of Jesus. Divine life! The power for overcoming is in this blood.

Exodus 5:1 And afterward Moses and Aaron went in, and told Pharaoh, Thus saith the

LORD God of Israel, Let my people go, that they may hold a feast unto me in the wilderness.

It was after the blood that Pharaoh left them. Every pharaoh that does want to leave you is about to leave by the power of the blood of the lamb. Exodus 12 chapter shows us the power of the blood of the lamb. JESUS is still as powerful today to deliver you from every marine power. Even if Pharaoh pursues you, the arm of the LORD is so strong that it overthrows the horse and its riders. No weapon shall destroy you.

Exodus 11:4 And Moses said, Thus saith the LORD, About midnight will I go out into
the midst of Egypt:

Amazingly, Passover happened in Exodus chapter 12. And again, the LORD about midnight went before them. Midnight is 12 too. 12 is a special number to GOD. JESUS walked with 12 Apostles. There are 12 tribes of Israel. 12 gates in the third heaven. 12 doors whereby the names of the Apostles are written. Apostle Peter couldn't continue in ministry before they found an Apostle to fill the space of Judas Iscariot. 12 is the number of completions.

At the end of this chapter, I will include blood prayer for destroying demonic powers. We plead the blood, speak the blood scriptures, and apply it to situations to change. You may be seeking deliverance from stagnation, poverty, or demonic ties of ancestral powers, the blood can deliver you.

Prayer points.

I stand on the ground of the blood of Jesus to proclaim victory over sin, Satan and his agents and the world.

I apply the blood of Jesus to every stubborn problem in my life.

I plead the blood of Jesus upon my body -from the top of my head to the sole of my feet.

I soak my life in the blood of JESUS.

I paralyse all satanic oppressors delegated against me with the blood of JESUS.

I apply the blood of the lamb over my soul, spirit and body in the name of JESUS.

My subconscious mind is covered with the blood of JESUS.

My will, emotions and feelings are covered with the blood of JESUS CHRIST.

I hold the blood of JESUS as a shield against any power that is already poised to resist me, in the name of JESUS.

By the blood of JESUS, I stand against every device of distraction.

I stand upon the word of GOD and I declare myself unmovable, in the name of JESUS.

By the blood of the lamb, every marine priest shall fall in the name of JESUS!

By the power of the blood of the Lamb I cover my family, my house and my land with the blood.

The blood of the lamb speaks better things in my finances than the blood of the Abel.

The blood of the lamb speaks better things over my career in the name of JESUS.

The blood of the lamb speaks better things over my health in the mighty name of JESUS!

Through the blood of JESUS, no weapon formed against me shall prosper.

My right ear, my right thumb, and my right toe is covered by the blood of JESUS CHRIST just like the priest Aron.

I hear and I see in spirit because of the covering of the blood of the lamb over my life.

My walk with CHRIST is energized and intensified by the power of the blood.

Like the Angel of the end time, my right foot is on the land, my left foot is on the sea, and my right hand up in the sky, and every territory of mine is covered by the blood of the precious CHRIST.

I am strong in the LORD by his precious blood.

The weapons of my warfare are not carnal but spiritual and mighty in the LORD.

Through the blood of Jesus, I have been redeemed out
of the hands of the devil.

I walk in the light and the blood of Jesus cleanses me from all sins.

Through the blood of JESUS, I am justified, sanctified and made holy with GOD's holiness.

Through the blood of JESUS, I have the life of GOD in me.

Through the blood of JESUS, I have access the presence of the LORD.

Let the blood of the Cross stand between me and any dark power delegated against me.

I curse every work of darkness in my life to dry to the roots by the blood of Jesus.

I draw a circle of the blood of Jesus around me.

I draw the blood line of protection around my property.

I overcome you Satan by the blood of the Lamb.

You cannot put any sickness on me because I am redeemed by the blood of the Lamb.

Let the blood of Jesus speak confusion into the camp of the enemy.

Let the blood of Jesus speak destruction unto every evil growth in my life.

Let the blood of Jesus speak disappearance unto every infirmity in my life.

Fasting and prayer as weapons.

We now come to the subject of prayer and fasting—one of the greatest spiritual principles of our time to silence the works of the enemy. Many do fast but lack prayer principles. When you are dealing with marine spirits, prayer, and fasting will strengthen your spirit man to fight even in your dreams when asleep as they penetrate your dream life.

When a man's prayer is weak, it is due to these cruel spirits of the water assigned for distraction. Often when you are about to pray, or in the middle of the prayer, a phone may ring or somebody may just knock at the door. These are some of the tricks they do to keep your fire down. Even at church when their anointing is starting to manifest, you will hear children starting to cry disturbing the service.

We are not to be ignorant of the devices of the enemy. The Devil wants a church that is sleep. He attacks ministers of the gospel with marine agents—using beautiful attractive women with deceitful charms to flirt with the pastor. A Pastor may not be interested but spirits behind the lady like a magnet will lure him to her. That's why these days there are so many sex scandals within the body of CHRIST.

As someone who has been living a fasted and prayerful life, I can attest to the power of prayer and fasting. Fasting and prayer deepen your spirit of discerning, you will no longer go about your soulish behavior when making serious decisions in your life.

Ephesians 1:3 Blessed be the God and Father of our Lord Jesus Christ, who hath blessed
us with all spiritual blessings in heavenly places in Christ:

The weapons of GOD are spiritual, not carnal. Fasting is a gift from GOD for us to humble our souls before Him. After humility comes exaltation. GOD honors the upright in heart. We have all spiritual blessings that are in heaven, not "some" spiritual blessings. It means that our walk should be the walk of authority and power.

Ephesians 1:18 The eyes of your understanding being enlightened;
that ye may know
what is the hope of his calling, and what the riches of the glory of his inheritance
in the saints,
19 And what is the exceeding greatness of his power to us-ward who
believe, according to the working of his mighty power,

The eyes of your understanding being enlightened, is the work of the Holy Spirit dropping your information in times of need. The power of the Holy Spirit that opens the spiritual portal of information to flow through you—walking in wisdom, word of knowledge, and understanding of spiritual matter like Daniel.

As a warrior of the LORD, your spirit must sense when there are angels or demons around. We all know that the spirit of GOD is a spirit of liberty and peace. Other spirits bring confusion and fear. If you are overwhelmed by fear, it is the workings of the demons.

Thus, I am proposing the fasting and prayer life. GOD will reward you. It is not in vain when you sacrifice your life for the kingdom of GOD. You reap what you sow. It is through fasting that we have the most effective means for taming the flesh and bringing the body under submission so that we may operate and minister in spiritual realms.

"Howbeit this kind goeth not out but by prayer and fasting"
(Matthew 17:21).

This is JESUS after the Apostle failed to cast out a demon out of a young man. There are some seasons where prayer itself would not be enough but fasting is. Prayer coupled with fasting can produce great results. Evil powers are destroyed. Marine Spirits' assignments are cut off. Poverty loses its power. The light shines in the darkness when serious prayers are offered from the place of authority.

The prayer of a righteous man can change the nations. You also can do great exploits in the kingdom of GOD, if you can be the student of the Word and work out your GOD-given faith. Faith as small as a mustard seed moves mountains.

Fasting is the greatest weapon that brings fire upon your body, which is the Holy Ghost anointing. While also bringing fire upon the kingdom of darkness—undoing the demonic ties that were assigned to your life.

The fast that God chooses is the one that brings liberty to the captive and helps the needy. When this type of fasting is sincerely employed, the results are almost staggering. The Christian is strengthened with might in the inner man...capable of waging spiritual warfare with great power...with this kind of testimony behind it:

When dealing with water spirits, you have to be violent in your prayers. You are in warfare, when there is war there is shaking happening. As the Children of the MOST HIGH, we have the sword of the spirit—which is the Word of GOD. Wear your warrior armor with dignity. Take the helmet of salvation, breastplate of righteousness, and cover your feet with the gospel of peace, and the shield of faith. I realize that this is what you need when you're dealing with principalities and powers. There are many fallen spirits and demons in the water realm.

Ephesians 6:10 Finally, my brethren, be strong in the Lord, and in the power of his
might.
11 Put on the whole armour of God, that ye may be able to stand against the
wiles of the devil.
12 For we wrestle not against flesh and blood, but against principalities,
against powers, against the rulers of the darkness of this world, against spiritual
wickedness in high places.

Everything we do has to be done in the name of the LORD. In the LORD there is power and might of His spirit upon our lives. His spirit works righteousness in our lives. Apostle Paul in this scripture emphasizes the word "Stand" meaning you have to be strong and courageous in your faith walk having the same attitude CHRIST had.

The armor of GOD is our defensive and attacking mechanism against the wiles of the devil. The scripture says "*He hath clothed me with the garment of salvation, he hasth covered me with robe righteousness*".

Isaiah 61:10 I will greatly rejoice in the LORD, my soul shall be joyful in my God; for

he hath clothed me with the garments of salvation, he hath covered me with the
robe of righteousness, as a bridegroom decketh himself with ornaments, and as a
bride adorneth herself with her jewels.

Satan fights you in spirit as he is a spirit being. And you are a spirit being first, and GOD has clothed you with the garment of salvation for believing in Him. This is the robe of righteousness that heavenly angels wear. In spirit, your soul and spiritual body are covered with the light of the glory of GOD. And the degree of light is measured by your holiness. Being holy, means you are set apart for a special survival for the LORD.

Above all, these clothes are your protective shield in the spirit world. The enemy has nothing to accuse you of when you are decked with clothes from the LORD. Especially when you are dealing with principalities and great fallen princes. Not that, principalities are not demons but fallen angels of great authority and power.

Only the light of God upon your lives can make them go. If you are pale in spirit, they are going to mess with you. And they have the right to do so. When you live in sin, is a doorway to the demonic activities to make your body their home.

The great price you can pay is to believe GOD and JESUS CHRIST. Faith is the greatest shield to quench the fiery darts of the enemy. And silence the evil arrows thrown at us day and night.

Psalm 91:5 Thou shalt not be afraid for the terror by night; nor for the arrow that
flieth by day;

Power over marine Prayer (Prayer Rain).

1. Any witchcraft practiced under any water against my life, receive immediate judgment of fire, in the name of Jesus.

2. Let every evil altar under any water upon which certain evils are done against me, be roasted, in the name of Jesus.

3. Every priest ministering at any evil altar against me inside any water, fall down and die, in the name of Jesus.

4. Any power under any river or sea remotely controlling my life, be destroyed by fire, and I shake myself loose from your hold, in the name of Jesus.

5. Let any evil monitoring mirror ever used against me under any water, crash to irredeemable pieces, in the name of Jesus.

6. Every marine witchcraft that has introduced spirit husband/wife or child in my dreams be roasted by fire, in the name of Jesus.

7. Every agent of marine witchcraft posing as my husband, wife or child in my dreams, be roasted by fire, in the name of Jesus.

8. Every agent of marine witchcraft physically attached to my marriage to frustrate it, fall down and perish now, in Jesus' name.

9. Every agent of marine witchcraft assigned to attack my finances through dream, fall down and perish, in the name of Jesus.

10. I pull down every stronghold of bewitchment, enchantment, jinx or divination fashioned against me by marine witches, in Jesus' name.

11. Let the thunderbolts of God locate and destroy every marine witchcraft covens where deliberations and decisions have ever been fashioned against me, in the name of Jesus.

12. Any water spirit from my village or the place of my birth, practising witchcraft against me and my family, be amputated by the word of God, in the name of Jesus.

13. Let every spiritual weapon of wickedness fashioned against me under any river or sea, be roasted by the fire of God, in the name of Jesus.

14. Any power of marine witchcraft holding any of my blessings in bondage, receive the fire of God and release them, in Jesus' name.

15. I loose my mind and soul from the bondage of marine witches, in the name of Jesus.

16. Any marine witchcraft chain binding my hands and feet from prospering, be broken and shattered to pieces, in Jesus' name.

17. Every arrow shot into my life from under any water by witchcraft powers, come out of me and go back to your sender, in the name of Jesus.

18. Any evil material transferred into my body through contact with any marine witchcraft agent, be roasted by fire, in the name of Jesus.

19. Every sexual pollution of marine spirit husband/wife in my body, be flushed out by the blood of Jesus.

20. Any evil name given to me under any water, I reject and cancel it with the blood of Jesus.

21. Every image constructed under any water to manipulate me, be roasted by fire, in the name of Jesus.

22. Any evil ever done against me through marine witchcraft oppression and manipulation, be reversed by the blood of Jesus.

SCRIPTURES CONCERING WATER SPIRITS

Psalm 74:13-14
Isaiah 27:1
Job 41:15
Psalm 18:40
Job 41:25
Psalm 89:10
Jeremiah 50:38
Psalm 104: 26

Notes

Bern Zumpano, *How To Perform An Effective, Lasting Deliverance or Self-Deliverance*, Word of Faith Ministries International, The School of Ministry

Self-Deliverance Prayer W/ Demon List To Cast Out! By Deliverance Revolution.org

Prayer Rain. *The Most Powerful And Practical Prayer Manual Ever Written* By DR D.K Olukoya.

Ojo Peter Korede. *Total Victory Over Marine Kingdom.*

Morris Cerrulo. You Can Know How To Defeat Satan: A Spiritual strategy Of Victory.

https://www.outofthedarknessbooks.com/post/are-you-held-back-by-marine-spirits

Don't miss out!

Visit the website below and you can sign up to receive emails whenever Johannes Tefo publishes a new book. There's no charge and no obligation.

https://books2read.com/r/B-A-UEZX-HKVZC

BOOKS2READ

Connecting independent readers to independent writers.

Did you love *Battle In The Sea: How To Tackle Spiritual Warfare And Win The Battle*? Then you should read *Deliverance From Mind Control: Be Free And Delivered From Every Marine Demons Of Mind Control*[1] by Johannes Tefo!

[2]

Free yourself from every evil mind controlling power in the name of Jesus. This book will help you to recognise evil powers of darkness that are targeting your mind and strategies to overcome powers of darkness by the blood of Christ. Christ overcame it, and you are liable to overcome it. We are heading into times where global mind control will be implemented to control the masses; don't be a victim. There is more power than the power

---

1. https://books2read.com/u/bx9DAe

2. https://books2read.com/u/bx9DAe

of this world, and that power is the power of the Holy Ghost to deliver the captives. Be delivered!

Also by Johannes Tefo

Family spiritual Warfare Books
Youth's Guide To Spiritual Warfare
A Women's Guide To Spiritual Warfare

Standalone
Deliver Your Soul From Evil
Overcoming Spirit Of Stagnation
The 24: Prophetic Word For This Season 2024 And Beyond
Michael For Warfare
Territorial Spirits: Overcome Evil Strongholds in Your Life And
Take Over Your Community With Strategic Warfare And
Winning Prayers
Prayers Against Suicide Spirit
Spiritual Warfare When Enough is Enough
Identity In Christ
Prayers Against Satanic Networks
The Workplace You Need: Spiritual Warfare Prayers That
Silence Evil Powers At Your Workplace.

Deliverance From Mind Control: Be Free And Delivered From Every Marine Demons Of Mind Control
Times Getting Hard: Scriptures Of Comfort For Hard Days
Battle In The Sea: How To Tackle Spiritual Warfare And Win The Battle

About the Author

Before he started writing Christian books, Johannes got a graduate degree in Film and Television from university of Johannesburg. After that, just to shake things up, he went to equip himself with religious studies, particularly Christianity, just to have knack about the world beyond the curtains of time. And how this body of Christ has transformed millions of people around the world, not neglecting how sadly the movement has been persecuted from time to time. He now writes full time.

www.ingramcontent.com/pod-product-compliance
Lightning Source LLC
Chambersburg PA
CBHW072107150726
47999CB00005B/1927